Memories of a Bootlegger's Daughter

Best Wishes
Your Enjoy
Leona V. (Schelske) Dietz

Memories of a Bootlegger's Daughter

Leona V. Pietz

ISBN: 978-1-57579-379-5

Library of Congress Control Number: 2008927997

Printed in the United States of America

PINE HILL PRESS
4000 West 57th Street
Sioux Falls, SD 57106

I dedicate this book to my extended family and to the memory of my parents, Adolph and Emelia Schelske and my Grandparents, Gottfried and Magdalena Schelske.

Thanks and Acknowledgements

Thanks to my daughter, Sharon, for her encouragement in writing my story, and for typing and editing it.

Thanks to my son-in-law, Derald, for his suggestions and for being a sounding board as we developed the story.

And thank you to every one who encouraged me to get my story down on paper.

A Little about the Author
Leona Veona (Schelske) Pietz

I was born in 1917 to Adolph and Emelia (Schnabel) Schelske. We lived east of Parkston, SD, on a farm. I attended grades one through eight in a one room schoolhouse. I grew up learning the farming life and the boot-legging life.

When I was twenty-one years old I married Theodore Pietz. We had two children, a son named Dale and a daughter named Sharon.

The early years of our married life were spent in Minnesota, Mitchell, SD, and Howard, SD. It was while we lived in Howard that we lost our son to a congenital disease. Soon after that we moved to Richmond, California where my husband, Ted, worked in the ship yard building ships for the war effort. I worked as a waitress.

Leona on her 90th Birthday

After three years we moved back to South Dakota on a farm near Tripp, SD. We farmed for twenty years.

Then there was a move to Rapid City, SD, where I worked as a waitress and Ted worked as a maintenance man.

At the end of ten years we moved back to Parkston, SD, back to my roots. I was then employed by Raven Industries, a sewing plant. I worked there for twenty years. When I reached the age of eighty I retired from Raven Industries. Since then I have been sewing quilts for my family and writing two books of my memoirs.

I am now ninety-one years old and I want to share a part of my life history with you. The things I talk about in this book are about a time and a way of life long gone. I tell my story as a way of preserving a piece of history. Though some may not condone my father's bootlegging activities it is nonetheless a part of history. This is the story of my experiences as a bootlegger's daughter.

Table of Contents

Foreword

The years of 1920 through 1933 were the "prohibition years." During those years it was illegal to consume or to produce distilled spirits or wine. Prior to that time Americans had the freedom to consume alcohol if they wished.

People who favored prohibition and the passage of the Volstead Act believed that alcohol was the cause of many of the social ills in America. Their hope was that jails, slums, alcoholism etc. would be wiped from the scene if alcohol was abolished.

By 1933, it was evident that prohibition was not working and the law was repealed.

Statistics show that alcohol consumption did go down for a period of time right after the prohibition law was passed. However, soon people found many sources for obtaining liquor.

Throughout the US many thousands of people produced their alcohol in stills in their basements, sheds, barns, in the woods, or under bridges. Many, many people were arrested for prohibition crimes. The punishment was either a fine or jail time. Most of these people served jail time because they could not come up with the money to pay the fines that were levied.

Liquor was also smuggled in from Canada, Mexico and Europe.

Many people who made and sold liquor were doing it to supplement other income during the hard times. Unfortunately there was some adulterated and even poisonous alcohol made.

"Moonshine," "Moonshine Whiskey," these were terms that became popular during prohibition. For secrecy, anyone who made liquor at home did it mostly at night under cover of darkness, in the light of the moon. The men who set up stills to make the whiskey were called "moonshiners" or bootleggers.

"Revenuers!" That was a word that struck fear into the hearts of the moonshiners. "Revenuers" were the Federal Revenue Agents who were responsible for enforcing the prohibition laws. They searched out the illegal activities of the moonshiners. They would descend on any home or farm where they suspected someone was making liquor. They would make surprise visits to these places and search them. If any stills, liquor or liquor making equipment was found they would destroy it. They could also arrest and/or fine the people.

Many of us have a stereotype in mind when we hear the words "moonshine."

We think of the hills and mountains of some of the southern states. Not so! During prohibition moonshining was going on around Parkston, SD.

This is where the story starts of Adolph Schelske's moonshine business and my part in it.

The Story

Come listen to the story I tell
I remember it all very well
The successes that we had
And the things that went bad
Come listen to the story I tell

Come listen to the story I tell
It may make you smile
As I tell of a time that's
Been gone for a long, long while
Come listen to the story I tell

Come listen to the story I tell
I tell how it was as I grew
Laughter, tears, lots of work
All those things we went through
Come listen to the story I tell

By Sharon Schnabel

I. Coming to America

I'm sitting here thinking of my childhood and the very difficult days for my Grandparents. Survival was so very difficult when they first came to America.

My grandfather told me stories of when he came to America from Russia. He got on a ship to come to America, not knowing a soul and not knowing if they would survive this deep, deep ocean voyage in an old ship. How much courage that must have taken. Everyone was

Gottfried and Magdalena Schelske, my Grandpa and Grandma Schelske, who played a big part in my life

praying for God's help and for everyone to pitch in and help keep it afloat. There were many people who took sick on the journey; some were ailing before the voyage began. They were told that if they died during the trip they would be tossed overboard. Grandpa said the reason for them to throw any dead bodies overboard was that the bodies would start smelling and the sharks would go crazy trying to get to the dead corpse. They could overturn the ship. All passengers were accounted for.

There was a young woman who delivered a baby on board. When the baby died the woman tried to keep it a secret. She wanted to be able to bury the baby in the ground when they arrived in the United States. To try to keep her secret, she wrapped and wrapped the baby with all the cloth she could find. However, after some time, a really strong odor became evident. Sharks were circling and rocking the ship. Everyone was terrified that the ship would go over. After much searching the smelly bundle was found and was thrown overboard.

The journey continued for some time and finally they reached land. They arrived in America, not knowing if there would be food to eat.

2.
Arriving in Parkston

After traveling through many states and looking at a lot of different places, Grandpa arrived in Parkston, SD. When he saw the town and the land around Parkston he decided this was where he would try to make his new home.

Parkston had been in existence only a short time and there were very few houses in the town when Grandpa first came to Parkston. In the countryside around Parkston there were only a handful of families living on the prairie, but sod was being broken and crops planted with horse drawn machinery.

Grandpa said it was a terribly hard time. When he first arrived in Parkston he worked at various odd jobs. He did a lot of hunting and fishing for food to eat.

After some time here, Grandpa met Magdalena Schulz. Magdalena had come to America from Russia when she was eight years old. She and her family lived in Milltown Township east of Parkston. Grandpa married Magdalena in 1890.

During those early years people could obtain free land through the Homestead Act and through the Homestead Act the government would give an individual one hundred and sixty acres of land if they agreed to "prove it up." They could have the land but they had to show good intent by putting buildings on the land and breaking the sod.

This sod house is very similar to Grandpa and Grandma's sod house

Grandpa and Grandma decided to take advantage of the Homestead Act. They began looking for land that would be good for growing crops.

My Grandpa chose some land southeast of Parkston. The land had rolling hills and a large creek running through it. That creek, later, came to play a big role in my Father's bootlegging. But my Grandpa had no thoughts of anything like that when he chose the land. He and my Grandma began improving their one hundred and sixty acres. They built a four room sod house. The house consisted of a kitchen, living room, bedroom and a porch or entry way. My Grandma told about building the sod house by carving blocks of sod out of the ground. The sod blocks were approximately ten inches long, five inches wide and three to four inches deep. These blocks were then stacked up to form walls.

They raised a family on the same land where I was later born. Their family consisted of two boys and two girls. One of those boys was my Father, Adolph.

Adolph and his brother, August, got into mischief sometimes. If Grandpa was not home the boys were forbidden to go up in the hayloft of the barn which had been built some time after the sod house was built. One nice fall day, Grandpa hitched the horses to the buggy, Grandma got in and they left to go into town. Adolph and August were left at home with some chores to do. When they finished their chores they decided they would go up in the hay loft. They were having so much fun playing up there, they forgot about the time. August had just gone down from the loft, when he heard the horses and buggy coming into the yard. Adolph was still up in the loft, what could he do? If he came out the front way, Grandpa would see him but August had an idea. He suggested that Adolph go to the other end of the loft where there was another door but no steps and there was a big swatch of grass on the ground and Adolph could jump down on that. August was the older of the two boys and Adolph trusted his judgment, so he took August's advice. He took a run and jumped down on the grass. He said he didn't think it was that far down to the ground and the swatch of grass he landed on was really not much of a swatch, it was more like just a few blades of grass. He wasn't sure he could even get to his feet. But for sure if he didn't get up and get away from there, he would get a spanking. He managed to get up and thankfully he didn't have any broken bones.

Another day Adolph and August were watching Grandma butcher geese and the boys had a brainstorm of an idea. Grandma would cut off the wings and throw them into the garbage and the boys gathered up the wings and went to the hay loft again. They were going to fly like birds! They got a ball of twine and tied the wings on their arms. They took a run and jumped out the door, but they forgot to flap their wings and they fell to the ground like a rock. Somehow they managed to not break their necks or anything else.

Adolph grew to adulthood and married Emelia Schnabel in 1914. They continued to work the land that Grandpa had homesteaded; there was still sod to be broken. They built a two-story frame house near the sod house where Grandpa and Grandma lived. My three brothers and I grew up in that house.

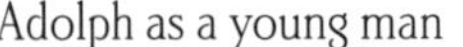

Adolph as a young man

Emelia as a young lady

Adolph and Emelia's house

As I was growing up, I spent as much time at the sod house as I did at my own house, as I spent a lot of time with Grandma and Grandpa. Our house was close enough to Grandpa and Grandma's house that during the summer if I was outside, I could smell what Grandma was cooking. If it was something I liked I was over to their house like a flash. One of the really good things that Grandma cooked was sweet sauerkraut. When I smelled that I always went to investigate and of course, Grandma would ask me to stay and have some. They usually had their noon meal around 11:30 so I could eat there and still get back to my house in time for the noon meal, which was usually served at 12:00. I had the best of two worlds because both my Grandma and my Mom were great cooks.

I helped in Grandma's garden and I listened to Grandpa's stories of coming to America. One job that Grandma gave me to do was to rid the garden of the gophers that bothered her plants. I would drown them out, kill them, and cut off their tails. I collected the tails and saved them in a box. When I had a lot of them I would take them to Grandma and she would give me a nickel for every tail. A nickel for every tail, I was rich!!

I also remember that Grandma had a huge Christmas cactus that hung in one of the windows of the sod house. That plant was so big! It was as wide as the window and nearly as long as the window. I dearly loved that plant. When it was blooming, I thought it was the most beautiful thing I had ever seen. I loved touching it.

Their house with its' thick earthen walls was a great place in the summer. It stayed so cool in there during the hot summer days.

Grandma and I did a lot of fishing together. We would go out in a small boat on the creek. That was great fun. Grandma liked to get up early and go out and fish. The getting up early wasn't such great fun though. I liked it better when we went fishing in the afternoon. Usually we caught enough fish for both families and Grandma would be the one to clean them. I wasn't too good about doing that.

I always liked to have Grandpa measure me to see if I grew. He would take a long piece of string to measure my height and mark it by tying a knot. I would take the string home for safe keeping. In a few days I would take my string back over to Grandpa so he could measure me again. I would ask Grandpa, "Did I grow?" Sometimes he would say yes and then we would have to move the knot. That always made my day.

My parents struggled to improve their lives. They worked hard, always hoping for a better future. As tractors and power machinery had not yet been invented they used horses and manual labor to work the land. When my Father took over the farm much of the land was still prairie and had to be turned over to be used for crops. My Father plowed the ground with the horses pulling the plow and him walking behind the plow.

There was so much hard manual labor. Everything was done by hand; shoveling snow with a hand scoop, pitching hay with pitch forks, carrying pails of water and feed for the animals, and using the horses and wagon for hauling things were all common place then.

The men hunted and fished to put meat on the table and the vegetables came from my Grandma's and my Mother's gardens.

Times were hard and money was short.

3. Hard Times

Drought, dust storms, grasshoppers and bank closings were the main causes of the hard times. When the drought hit, lakes and rivers dried up, the livestock on the farms was starving. Crops weren't growing and the pastures had no grass.

In the spring, we all had worked hard preparing the soil and planting the crops. Then we stood by, day after day waiting and waiting for rain. We would watch the sky hopefully for just the smallest cloud. But each day just seemed to get hotter and drier than the day before. There were no rain storms, just dust storms. The small grain, the corn and the prairie burned to a crisp. What would we do for feed for the animals during the coming winter? There were no crops to bring in from the fields. The only things that had grown were big thistles.

My Father decided that we were going to cut these fields of thistles and put them up into stacks, like hay stacks. The thistles were cut, my Mom raked them into windrows and my Dad gathered them and dumped them on a pile. At this time I was around twelve years old and my job was to be on the thistle stack and spread the thistles like you would a hay stack. Dad tried to cut the thistles as green as possible, then as we stacked them we sprinkled salt on them. We did this layer by layer, a layer of thistles, a covering of salt, another layer of thistles and more salt. The salt was put on to "cure" the green thistles so that when the cattle ate them they wouldn't get diarrhea.

How hot and miserable I was on the thistle stack. I wore heavy overalls and four buckle overshoes for protection from the thorny thistles. But some of the thorns went right through my overalls. By quitting time, my legs would be really raw and sore. Meanwhile the temperatures stayed hot and the hot dry wind continued to blow.

It seemed unbelievable that the livestock would even eat the thistles but they did because they were so hungry and there wasn't anything else to eat. One of the problems that developed from the cattle eating the thistles is that sometimes a thistle would get lodged in their mouth and begin to fester. They would develop open sores that had to be treated.

Another year, there was a little corn in the field that got big enough for Dad to cut with the corn binder. Mom and I shocked that into corn shocks and in the fall we hauled it home and Dad would run it through the corn shredder. The corn was a fancy treat for the livestock!

One hot, dry day in September of 1927, with the hot wind blowing, we were working in the hay field. It had been such a hot and dry summer and we had been hoping for rain for many days. The pastures were so dry there wasn't enough grass for the cattle. There was very little hay in the meadow but we cut what little there was. Dad, the hired man and I were working on hauling it home and stacking it when in the afternoon it started to get cloudy and we were hoping that it would finally rain. We watched the clouds as we were unloading a load of hay. It was 4:00 in the afternoon, the time when Mom would always have a lunch ready for us to eat. We stopped working, tied the horses to a post and were on our way up to the house. Dad took one more look at the sky. There was a bank of clouds in the northwest and another one in the southwest Dad said, "we don't want that one from the northwest, we want the one from the southwest." We had just finished our lunch when it began to hail badly. We ran for the horses, they were spooked, jumping around and trying to get away. We unhooked them as fast as we could and got them into the barn. Where ever the hailstones hit the ground the dust would puff up. My Dad got his wish, we had gotten the storm from the southwest. It hailed so much that the ground was covered and then we saw the tornado coming. We all ran for Grandpa's sod house because it would be safer than our frame house. We, no more than got into the sod house and the debris was flying all over in the yard. Grandpa's garage was demolished and his car was laying up side down. The tornado took off the top half of the horse barn and our side sheds. It tore up our big long haystack, tore out fences and uprooted large trees. And finally after all that we got some rain. But the hail and tornado had destroyed everything. It had pounded the grass into the ground and the little corn that we would have had was all shredded. My parents had worked all summer for nothing it seemed. They now had to rebuild and repair everything and think of winter on its way. The little hay that we had hauled in to be used for winter feeding had to be used now for the livestock. When winter came, Dad had to buy feed and haul it in to our farm.

During these hot, dry times the wind blew and we had big dust storms. The dust would blow through any little cracks in the house. We put wet rags on the window sills and below the doors to seal any openings where the dirt and dust could sift in. It was impossible to keep it out though. It would even sift into the beds. It would be gritty and grimy when you pulled back the covers.

The dust storms caused the ditches to fill with fine dust. The dust lay in drifts in the ditch, much like snow does. Each storm made the drifts grow a little higher.

One day it turned really dark in the northwest. We were so happy thinking it was finally going to rain. The closer the cloud got, the darker it got. It was almost as dark as night as we lit our kerosene lamps in order to see in the house. Then all of a sudden we heard a queer noise as the cloud was right by our farm. To our amazement, it was not rain, it was GRASSHOPPERS! It was a cloud of grasshoppers so thick that you couldn't see the sun. When they landed they ate everything in sight. They ate things down to the black dirt. They sat on the fence posts so thick that you couldn't see the posts at all. Before this "cloud" arrived someone had left a jacket hanging on a fence post. The grasshoppers even ate that! The only thing left was the buttons lying on the ground. In the following days during the hottest part of the afternoon they would sit on the shady side of the fence posts.

As well as covering the fence posts, the grasshoppers would cover the walls of the house and the barn. You would have had to see it to believe it.

They would eat a whole field of grain and then move on to the next field. There would be nothing left but black ground when they finished. This is something I have never forgotten in all my ninety-one years.

On that first day when the grasshoppers arrived, the cattle came running home with the grasshoppers plastered thick on their backs. They had never experienced anything like this before!

When you would walk along in the yard the grasshoppers would fly up and hit you in the face. It felt like sandpaper rubbing on your face.

These grasshoppers were huge. Dad caught and measured some of them. They were three inches long! He put them in a jar and took them to Parkston and they were put in one of the store windows for everyone to see.

There were even stories of trains being delayed because the tracks were made slippery by the crushed grasshoppers.

The government got involved in trying to get rid of the grasshoppers. Various studies were conducted. One method they came up with was to make bait which consisted of bran or sawdust treated with arsenic. This bait was distributed free to farmers.

Everyone was so desperate. Garden vegetables and potatoes were cooked in their jackets. No one would dream of wasting the peelings.

Every drop of water was used twice. Dishwater was saved for the pigs and the bath and laundry water was used in the garden.

Also during this time, my Father had a very bad experience with a bank. He had borrowed money and the mortgage was coming due. So he loaded a load of hogs and took them to the Morrell Stockyards in Sioux Falls and sold them. The next day he went to the bank that held the mortgage and paid it. He felt so good about having that taken care of. Shortly thereafter, he received a letter from the bank saying that his mortgage was due. Dad went right to the bank and told them that he had paid it. They insisted it wasn't paid and they asked for a receipt. He had paid cash and he hadn't asked for a receipt! He had no proof that he had paid it. They said, "it has to be paid." Dad came home that day in tears. I had never seen my Dad in tears before. We had no more livestock to sell except for the milk cows. My Dad said,"we will have to sell some of them," which is what was done to make the payment. He always made sure after that to ask for a receipt in all his business dealings.

How did everyone survive during this hard time? I think of the hardships my parents faced, not knowing how to feed the animals and the family day after day as the drought and grasshoppers continued. How did they have the courage, the stamina and the fortitude to keep going?

4. Becoming a Moonshiner

With all the setbacks and hardships, my Dad started planning a way to bring in a little more money to feed his growing family. By now there were four mouths to feed. I was seven years old and my brother was an infant.

During the years of prohibition, my Dad had been making liquor for just the family gatherings and celebrations and close friends' use, by using a large kettle on the stove. One must remember that a German-Russian tradition had come to America with the German-Russian immigrants. It had always been a tradition when you had meal time guests, to offer them a small drink before the meal. A small glass of homemade wine or something stronger was offered before everyone went to the table. So with the introduction of prohibition that custom became illegal. But many people continued it discreetly.

Some of the moonshine he made was used to treat colds and sicknesses. Toothaches were treated by taking a mouthful of the whiskey and holding it in your mouth until the jaw was numb. It was up to you then whether you wanted to swallow it or spit it out.

Dad began planning to do his moonshine production on a larger scale. He thought it would bring in a little more money and make life a little easier for the family.

Moonshining required many talents. A moonshiner had to have a lot of skill, knowledge, understanding and patience. It required hard work and cleanliness. He had to be a good judge of the character of a man and have a good sense of men to avoid the "revenuers." I saw my Dad display those characteristic many times. A moonshiner had to be sly as a fox, tight lipped, mindful of his own business and sworn to secrecy. This secrecy was drilled into me. I was warned over and over to not ever tell anyone anything about the moonshining things my Dad was doing.

As Dad planned his expansion he knew it would have to be a very secretive operation. Only a very limited number of people could know about his increased production of liquor. Neighbors could not know where he was making the liquor or even that he was making it.

How to do it? That was the puzzle my Dad worked on that winter. He decided that the best time to work on it would be at night when the neighbors were sleeping. He knew that if he was found out it would mean jail time. But he decided to take the risk.

My Grandparents were still living next door in the four-room sod house they had built on the farm. We lived in the frame house a stone's throw away. Even my Grandparents were not to know what he was doing. He did not want them involved in any way if the revenue agents should come and investigate.

5.
The New Hired Hand

During this time also a young man came to work on the farm. This young man, Ed, was attending high school in Parkston and was very involved in sports. He was an excellent football player as were his two friends, Walsh and Adkins. When he wasn't in school or practicing for football, he would come out to the farm to work. My Dad needed the help and Ed could use some extra money. My Dad always said he didn't know what condition Ed would be in when he arrived out at the farm; if he had been in some tough practices or tough football games, he wouldn't be in the best condition to work. Sometimes he had injuries from the cleats on the football shoes and his skin would be all torn up. Since he always treated me like his kid sister and tolerated me following him around, I felt so sorry for him when he showed up injured like that. My Dad had lots of patience with Ed and he would treat and bandage him up. Sometimes Ed would have a hard time walking but he always put forth a good effort. As I said before, my Dad had much patience with Ed and never overworked him. He would give him time to heal up. Basketball season wasn't as hard on Ed, so he didn't arrive out at the farm with so many injuries. Since his two friends and him were such good players, we went to see them play some of their games in Parkston.

Ed's Father was happy to have Ed working and learning on the farm. He said, "it kept Ed from running wild in town." It also was an opportunity for him to earn some money for college. Ed's Father was a carpenter and he was out at the farm sometimes too. When some buildings needed to be rebuilt after the tornado had hit our farm, he helped do that. He was generous enough to reduce his labor prices and he was patient about getting paid. He knew Dad would pay him as soon as he possibly could. I remember how long it would take to get a load of lumber using the horses and wagon. They had to travel all the way to Yankton to get it

Ed and his parents

With summer coming Ed would be out at the farm all the time. I was overjoyed to hear that. Little did I know that we would both be kept busy with the whiskey-making operation.

My Dad had started his underground liquor making for family and close friends in 1920. Everyone said he made the best tasting whiskey! That may have been another reason he decided to go into larger production. As his reputation grew for having quality whiskey, he increased his production. He began producing more and more to fill the requests of people who enjoyed his moonshine.

It became a family operation. My Father, Adolph, my Mother, Emelia, Ed and I, being seven years old, were all involved in the process. I was repeatedly coached to never, ever say anything to anyone about what we were doing. I became my Dad's little helper and Ed became his right-hand man. Because I idolized Ed, I would follow him around as he did various jobs and chores around the farm.

At night, I always told my Mom to have my clothes laid out for the morning because when I woke up, I would have to hurry to get dressed and get outside to "help" Ed. I told my Mom, "Ed is from town and he can use a lot of help until he knows how things are done." I was so delighted and proud to be helping like that.

One of the jobs that needed to be done involved maintaining the hiding places for the moonshine. Dad had created some hiding places along the fence lines of our property. He had made holes in the ground along the fence lines and then he made wooden boxes with lids and dropped them into the holes. Dirt was backfilled around the boxes and covered over the top of them.

With the horses and wagon, Ed and I worked along the fence line. We had to clean the boxes and make sure they were ready for use. I got to drive the horses for Ed just like I did for my Dad. Ed made me feel so important, saying he couldn't get the job done without me.

My Mother did her part in the kitchen, which involved cooking the flavoring to be added to the whiskey. A few other people assisted also. Three men, Fred, Dan and John, were the salesmen for the moonshine; they were the contacts for the customers. They never knew where the

Author rendered sketch of driving the horses for Ed when we cleaned the boxes along the fence line

alcohol they were selling came from. They didn't have knowledge of the location of the brewery or if Dad was just the middle man and was getting the moonshine from a third party.

Another one of Ed's responsibilities was to see that everything ran smoothly. He checked to be sure everyone knew their job, what to do, when to do it and how to do it. This had to be a very secretive operation. Everything had to be done in the dark of night so neighbors would not notice anything unusual going on. And of course, all the helpers had to be very close-mouthed and careful about what they said. No loose lips!

6. The Whiskey Making Process

The process of making the whiskey had several steps. Usually we worked with three barrels and then a certain amount of oats or barley was put in the barrel. Most often he used oats because that was what he had on the farm. Next some cakes of yeast and a large quantity of sugar went into the barrel and finally enough water was added to fill the barrel.

Dad would then cover the barrels with canvas to keep the contents clean and they were left for some time to ferment. Each day while it was fermenting each barrel would have to be stirred. You had to be careful as you stirred because as you stirred, gas bubbles would come up from the bottom of the barrel. If you were stirring too hard, the contents would bubble up over the sides of the barrel and you would lose some valuable product.

After it was done fermenting we would drain the barrels. The liquid went into the still. What remained was the mash and it would be discarded.

The still would heat the liquid to a certain temperature and then it was passed through a coil in a cooling container, which was filled with cold water

Then it was time to fill the jugs. If there wasn't an immediate order to fill, the whiskey would be poured into charcoal treated barrels to age, but occasionally there was an immediate order to fill. If that was the case the liquor was put in jugs and sold without aging.

Author rendered picture of wagon backed into the hollowed out area of the straw stack, where jugs and barrels would be hidden. The wagon would be driven out and the area covered over with straw after the jugs and barrels were hidden.

My Father worked very hard brewing moonshine during those nights. When he had a few barrels and jugs filled he would hitch the horses to the wagon and drive up and over the hill to where the straw stack was. A straw stack was a large mound of straw that had been blown by a threshing machine into an inverted cone shape. This straw was often used for spreading on the floors of the barns for the livestock to lie down on. However, that wasn't the only use of the straw stack on our farm. My Dad also used it as a hiding place for the moonshine. He would use a pitch fork and burrow deep into the pile and hide the jugs and barrels there.

Some nights on the wagon trip to the straw stack, I would get to ride along and even get to hold the reigns to guide the horses. I felt so important as I did that, not realizing that the horses, being very intelligent animals, knew the route to the straw stack and didn't really need any guiding from me. We would work until the wee hours of the night. Then we would go to the house where my Mom had a lunch ready for us. After that lunch, it was off to bed.

I remember going with my Dad one dark night when I was seven or eight years old and having this very serious talk with him. It was serious to me anyway. As I sat on the wagon seat next to him I said, "When I get bigger, I can help you make this 'stuff.' We will work together." As I got older, I did become my Dad's helper with brewing the whiskey up until the time he quit making it. After he quit moonshining, I continued to be his helper, but in a different way— I was his farm hand until I got married.

As I recall all this I realize what chances my Father took. It must have been a tremendous strain on my parents when the revenue agents appeared on the farm. The federal revenue agents had a hunch that some bootlegging was going on at the farm and they would appear periodically to search. There were times they would ask me questions. Because I had been repeatedly coached by my parents to never tell anything about what we were doing, I would not answer the revenue men. After repeatedly asking me questions and me not responding they may have thought that I was mute.

7. REVENUERS!!

As I stated before there were some men selling and taking orders and one day Fred, one of the sellers, had a big order for whiskey. My Dad told Fred that he could pick up his order down by the farm. He was to come in the south gate after sun down when it was dark. Shortly before it was time for Fred to pick up the moonshine, he began to have second thoughts about the transaction. He had sold to a total stranger. He realized that these strangers could possibly be Federal Revenue Agents. He decided that when the time came for him to meet with the strangers at the farm and deliver the moonshine to them he would tell them that he hadn't been able to get it for them.

Not knowing about Fred's misgivings my Dad and Ed were busily working at the straw stack, which was about one mile from our farm. They were uncovering the moonshine to fill the big order. While they were working at the straw stack, my Mother back at the farm was to get the horses hitched to the wagon, drive down to the straw stack and then bring the load of moonshine back to the farm where Fred and his buyers would pick it up. I'll never forget how badly I wanted to go with my Mom in the wagon that night. But she told me no and that I was to stay with Grandpa and Grandma at the sod house. I was so disappointed that I just cried a river. But no meant no and I stayed with Grandpa and Grandma. After Mom hitched the horses to the wagon she drove them through the dark night to the straw stack and she proceeded to help with the uncovering and loading the moonshine onto the wagon.

Meanwhile back at the farm, the strangers had arrived and Fred was telling them that he didn't have the moonshine for them because he didn't have the cash. They became very angry and upset and started shouting at Fred using all kinds of vulgar language, but Fred stuck to his story. They started to push and shove him around and that was when they told Fred that they were Federal Agents and pulled a gun on him. They told him that if he knew what was good for him, he'd better get with it. They pointed the gun right in his face. At that point, Fred lost it. He told them to just hold it and he would tell them where to go to find the moonshine. They said they had better directions and they would use their own judgment.

They took off in their vehicle through the north gate and off across the field in the direction of the straw stack. Driving as fast as they could, they bounced over the rough ground. As they got closer to the straw stack, they turned on their lights and they could see Dad, Mom and Ed uncovering the moonshine and loading it into the wagon. At that moment my Dad knew something was awfully wrong. He yelled for Mom and Ed to run for it! "Run into the cornfield. Run as fast as you can." They ran and then because the corn was not very tall, they dropped to their knees and crawled as fast as they could. The federal men stopped their car and ran for the cornfield too. They yelled for my Mom and Ed to come out of the field or they would shoot. Ed and Mom kept crawling along the corn rows as fast as they could. The federal men then started firing down and across the corn rows and running around like mad. They knew there were more people around but it was too dark to see anything in the cornfield and Ed and Mom kept crawling through that forty acre field and then through the pasture in the pitch darkness. Ed said the pellets, from the shot guns they were using sometimes came to close for comfort. That darkness saved them from being caught.

Back at the sod house it seemed like we heard the shooting for a long, long time. Grandpa and Grandma, of course, had no idea what could possibly be going on and why there were shots being fired. They must have been terrified.

While the revenue agents were shouting and running around crazily in the corn field, my Dad was holding on to the horses to keep them from running off across the field. With all the yelling and guns being fired the horses were frightened and were pawing the ground, jumping around trying to escape all the bedlam. If my Dad had not been holding on to them they would have bolted like a streak of lightning.

After giving up on catching the people in the cornfield the agents searched the straw stack looking for more moonshine but it had all been loaded onto the wagon. The revenuers removed the barrel of whiskey and the gallon jugs from the wagon and loaded them onto their vehicle. They then told my Father to follow them with his horses and wagon down to the farm. As he followed them with the horses and wagon, he was thinking "What a loss." He also knew the fine would be large. In those days there was no extra money. At the farm Dad was arrested and fined $100.00, which was a huge amount of money in those days. He did manage to scrape up the money though and avoided going to jail.

It was a good thing that my Mother and Ed were not found or caught because if they had been caught it would have meant two more fines and my parents would not have been able to come up with the money. That would have meant jail time for two of the people.

My Mom was so thankful that she had not allowed me to go with her. It all might have ended differently if I had been along. Most likely, Mom, Ed and I would have been caught because I would have slowed them down. I could have become the youngest bootlegger to do time in jail.

I think that it must have been an awful shock to my Grandparents when they saw the Federal Agents come into the yard followed by my Dad and then seeing him being arrested and possibly more shocking hear my Mother and Ed's story when they finally came to the house after the agents had taken my Dad and left. I'm sure it was a terrible night for them.

Grandpa in the farm yard

8. The Brewery in the Dug-Out

After his arrest and fine my Dad did not produce any moonshine for a couple of years. The Federal Agents were watching him too closely. They would appear often and unexpectedly to check on him. The vehicles they drove were Model A Fords, which they drove like race cars. They would always come flying over and down the hill in a big rush trying to have it be as big a surprise visit as possible. Whenever I would go outdoors to play my Mother always said, "Leona, be careful and watch out for the revenuers." If I had gotten in their way as they came flying down the hill, they might have run right over me.

However after a time, since there didn't seem to be any bootlegging activity going on at the farm, the revenue agents moved on to watching other people and they weren't keeping Dad under close surveillance anymore, though they did still make some surprise visits. That was when he decided he would start up his production again. He would build an underground cave, which he called a "dug-out."

Our farm was down in a valley. The creek ran along the south and east boundaries of the farm yard and to the north of the farm yard, there was a steep hill which was still native prairie. Above that hill, lay our farm ground which had been tilled. There was a road approximately one-half mile long leading up that hillside, with a fence on each side of the road. Just as you reached the farm ground, there was a ditch to cross and a gate to open before you got into the field. Southwest of the gate there was a lake bed that very seldom had water in it because it

In the foreground see the infamous creek that bordered the farm to the south-east. It was the disposal for the mash in all the operations. A sewer line piped the mash into the creek. The fish loved to feed on the mash and as a result we got many fish suppers from the creek

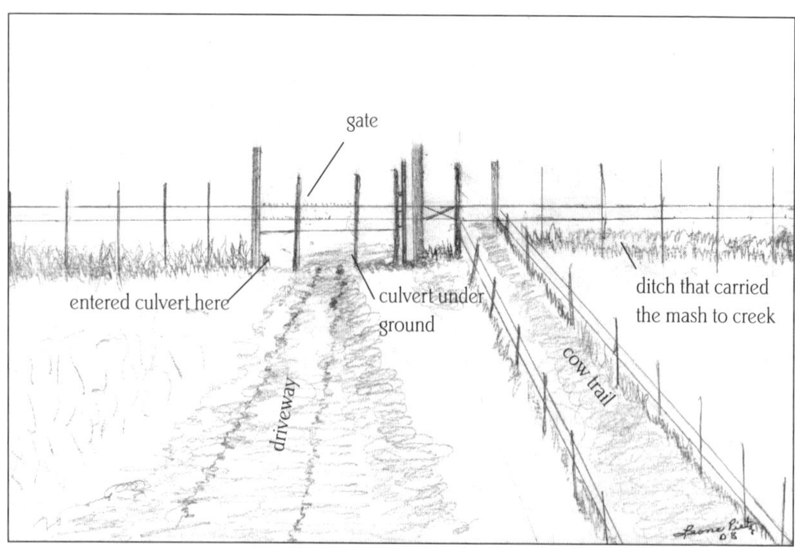

Author's rendering of the driveway, gate and culvert

had been ditched to drain to the east down to the creek. It was in this area that Dad decided to center his new area of production.

A deep cave or hole would be built in the center of the road under the gate where he would carry on his moonshine production. A large culvert would have to be placed so it would meet the ditch to the west and east and after it was in place it should appear that the sole purpose was the ditching of water down to the creek. Hopefully no one would suspect anything else was going on.

It was May of 1927, and school was closed for the summer break and Ed was still working on the farm as my Dad's "right hand man." Dad was eager to get started on digging the cave or "dugout" as they called it. Ed would be available all day during summer, instead of just before and after school as it was during the school year.

At that time, of course, there was no power equipment to use for this project. They used two horses pulling a scraper. One man ran the scraper and another man drove the horses. They scraped the hole approximately seven feet deep, ten feet wide and twelve feet long. With a great deal of hard work they got all the dirt excavated. They then used bridge planks for the walls and the ceiling. On the south side of this dugout, they also cleaned out dirt so that the large culvert could be laid there. The culvert would be covered over with dirt and just look like a place for the water to run through under the road.

They cut a hole in the middle along the side of the culvert. Dad made a square frame around the hole. This hole became a door through which they could take supplies into the dugout. Since that lake was dry most of the time, and this was during some very dry years, the culvert was also dry most of the time. There seemed to be no rain, just hot dry winds blowing nearly every day. They could enter the culvert at the end, crawl down to the middle and then through the doorway, they had made, into the dug out. This was the way they brought into the dugout the supplies they needed for making the moonshine. Sugar, grain and water were some of the supplies they carried in. The larger equipment, like the whiskey still and the barrels were taken into the dugout before the culvert was put in place.

The dugout and the culvert all had to be covered with dirt, making it as natural-looking as possible.

Inside the dugout, lanterns were used for lighting and supplies were hand-carried into the dugout. Water was brought in with pails and a long hose. Imagine crawling through the culvert carrying the supplies and water. What at job that must have been for the men.

I remember my Dad crawling into the culvert all the time to enter the dugout. I didn't go in anymore than I had to; I didn't like it in there. I wasn't a gopher! I liked the wide open spaces.

There was a lot of hard work until the mash was ready to be strained out. Mash is a by-product of the whiskey distilling process and is discarded. The mash was strained out of the brew and passed through a hose down through the culvert and on down to the creek. The fish loved the discarded mash. That area where the mash was dumped became a very good feeding ground for them and a good fishing hole for us. We caught some nice plump fish there.

(Left to right) Friend, Ed and Dad, during a day of hunting and fishing.

As time went on, the dirt would wash off or be blown off the top of the dugout and more dirt would have to be replaced. You could always tell when it was time to put more dirt in place. You could tell by the sound it made when you drove across it with the horses and wagon. If there wasn't enough dirt for insulation it would sound very hollow. More dirt would be placed on top. Also the ditches on either side of the road were cleaned and scraped to account for the new ground on the road, as there should be no indication of the dugout.

Brewing the whiskey at this location went on for about two years.

Then one summer day we had a terrific rain and hail storm. The lake bed and the ditches filled up with water. The water went over the banks of the lake and flooded the area. The dugout was filled with water. Everything was destroyed and that ended the moonshining in that location.

Interestingly, the Federal Agents had driven across the dugout many times, but never suspected anything. They were always in a hurry to get through the gate and down to the farm yard, thinking their surprise appearance would help them discover something. The revenuers were quite rude and disrespectful to everyone on the farm. Women were very afraid of the main two Federal Agents, who I will refer to as Mr. Y. and Mr. Z.

9. The Brewery in the Basement

There was also a time when my Father turned a room in the basement of our house into a place to brew whiskey. It was below the kitchen floor. The area was about fifteen feet square and was not visible when you were in the basement. There was a coal storage area and a bathroom in the basement and a secret door had been built along one wall with three shelves. These shelves appeared to be a storage area for fruits and vegetables. But the shelves were false and could be removed in order to enter the area where he brewed the whiskey. The sewer pipes from the bathroom went right through the brewing room so the mash was pumped right into the sewer. The drain field for the sewer went through the chicken yard. This was on a slant about one hundred feet from the house. The chickens loved to drink the water at the end of the sewer line. They sometimes became tipsy after drinking the water and pecking at the mash that came out of the sewer line. The first time my Mother saw the chickens acting all weird and not being able to walk very well, she was alarmed and thought they were sick. That could be a catastrophe because their eggs and the meat of the chickens was a big source of food for us. But shortly, Mom and Dad figured out what was really wrong with the chickens and they were quite relieved. Those drunken chickens in the chicken yard were a funny sight.

One day the Federal Agents made one of their surprise visits to the farm. One of the agents stood for a long time and looked at the sewer line in the chicken yard. Finally he asked Dad, "where does the water come from?" My Dad said, "from the downstairs toilet." Dad was quite uneasy for a time while the agent went downstairs and checked it out. After looking around in the basement, he seemed satisfied and went on his way, much to my Dad's relief. It was a good thing that the revenue agent hadn't been there on the day the chickens were drunk. Would he have figured it out?

There was also a trap door in the southeast corner of the kitchen that led down to the brewing room. It was a square hole just large enough to crawl through. The kitchen had wall to wall linoleum floor covering, which covered the trap door. There was an old fashioned cupboard on rollers that set over the trapdoor also. Whenever Dad wanted to go down, he would roll the cupboard ahead, lift the linoleum and crawl down. When he was down there, it was my responsibility to watch the driveway. The drive way was approximately five blocks long with a gate at the entrance. I was to let him know when any car would turn into the driveway and it was a job that I hated because it was so boring. When a car would enter the driveway, the dogs would bark. I always felt like a watch dog too. I would race to the house to warn Dad. "Hurry and come up there's a car at the gate!" I would yell. The gate was always closed. Anyone in a vehicle coming to the yard, would have to open the gate, drive through, close the gate and then drive up the driveway. That would give Dad enough time to climb up through the trap door, lay down the linoleum and put the cupboard back in place. Believe me, when I say, "things were really moving" as Dad came up from the basement at those times.

In the early days there were a lot of salesmen that went from farm to farm. There were "Watkins" salesmen with their wares of flavorings for cooking and there were the "McNess" salesmen with their products who came to sell to the farm women. If the farm women didn't have enough cash to pay for the products they wanted, the salesmen would often take live chickens in trade. For the men there were salesmen selling magazines or selling horses. There were also farmers going back and forth to help each other. So if I saw any of the salesmen or neighbors at the gate, I would have to quickly let my Dad know.

My fathers' salesmen were busy selling moonshine. Dad had some private customers he would sell whiskey to. One situation that sticks out in my mind was the case of the two bachelors who lived near Dimock and were both very good customers. However, if Dad would stop at their home when they both were home, he couldn't sell them anything. But Dad found that if he stopped at their house when just one or the other was there, he could sell quite a large amount. It was amusing. Neither brother wanted the other to know that he was buying moonshine.

Some other good customers were Mr. and Mrs. J. and they always paid cash. After receiving the moonshine, the husband would always tell his wife, "Mama, go and get the man some money and pay him." Dad said he was sure they hid their money in the flour sack because the bills they gave him always had a white film on them.

He also found that some of his male farm customers hid their money in the machine shed or tool shed among the tools.

10. Trying His Hand at Beer-Making

My Father also tried his hand at making beer just for our own use. The first batch was a joke. He did everything right from the malt and settling, then to adding the sugar, and finally to bottling and capping it. It would have to set for a few days and then be ready to drink.

One evening we had company. Everyone was sitting around playing cards, talking and laughing. Every now and again there was a popping sound coming from the basement. What had happened was that Dad had added too much sugar which formed too much pressure and the bottles were exploding. The caps were being blown right off the bottles. He managed to save only a few bottles. It was even dangerous to hold the bottle, because you never knew when it might explode.

His second batch of beer was fine. He followed the recipe closely and took great care when he added the sugar. It was a great refreshment during the hot weather when working on the farm.

11.
The Third and Last Brewery

As my Dads' moonshine business expanded and the quality of his whiskey became known in places as far away as Chicago, he needed a bigger place to brew the whiskey, as there was a demand and a market for his whiskey.

With a bigger brewing operation Dad needed more help with the farming. Ewald was hired to work on the farming. He was not involved with the whiskey making and somehow he never knew that the whiskey making was going on. He worked hard all day in the fields and at night he fell into bed and slept through the night activities happening on the farm. Dad didn't want Ewald to have any knowledge of the brewing operation so that there would never be any repercussions for him. If the revenue agents questioned Ewald he could honestly say he knew nothing about any moonshining. There was a big barn on the

Ewald

farm that Dad used as a workshop for overhauling engines and doing repairs for other people along with the workshop there was a blacksmith shop. My Dad would sharpen sickles for grass mowers for himself and for customers. With that I had another job, holding the long end of the sickle while he sharpened the blade at the other end. That seemed to be an everlasting job for me. I'm sure my Dad never overworked me, but I was so glad when it was finished for the season.

He decided to put a basement under the cement floor of this barn. That would become the new brewing area, which was his biggest one yet.

He and Ed did the digging again using the horses and the scraper. They excavated an area about thirty feet square. Having learned from the flooding of the "dugout" they reinforced this hole with cement. The walls were made of cement and planks. He put a wall through the basement, making an area about ten by fifteen foot with a stairway leading down to it. That area was open to the public. The room on the other side of the wall was the new brewing area. This was at a time when there was no Rural Electric Association (REA) furnishing electricity to the farms. So my Dad set up his own electric power for the farm. He put in a sixteen bottle Delco light plant which produced thirty-two volts of electricity. That light plant furnished the electricity for the farm and for the brewing area on the other side of the wall. This time there were electric lights instead of kerosene lanterns for lighting the brewing area. The room also had a large stove to heat the work shop and an underground pipe that took heat over to the brewing area.

His method of making a secret entrance to the brewing area was rather unusual. On the main floor he built a bathroom which was approximately six by eight feet. Next to the bathroom he built some false shelves that he kept tools on. There was a hollow area where he ran a pipe under the shelves. The pipe had a chain attached to it. The other end of the chain attached to the floor. There was also a crank and the crank could be turned to wrap the chain around the pipe and raise or lower a part of the bathroom floor that was hinged. The commode set on that part of the floor so when the floor was lowered, the stool set at a downward angle. This then was the secret trapdoor for entering the brewing room. When the trap door was closed it gave the appearance of just being an ordinary commode in the bathroom. Again there was a sewer line that took the mash down to the creek.

In the brewing room he set up a hundred gallon upright steel tank, which was to be the pressure tank for the mash. The tank was heated to a certain temperature for brewing. Next to the pressure tank was a wooden livestock watering tank filled with cold water. There was a coil that wound round and round in that tank. The alcohol was cooled as it ran through the coil. It was then ready to be put in jugs or other containers. He had twelve-fifty gallon barrels for the mash with canvas covers.

If rye and oats was used for the mash, it only cost thirty-five cents to brew a gallon and we sold it for $1.50. In the depth of the depression $1.50 was a lot of money.

The supplies which consisted of oats, rye, corn, barley, yeast and sugar, was rolled into the brewing area. We needed a lot of sugar and that would be delivered out to the farm from one of the stores in Parkston. The delivery man never asked any questions when he delivered the sugar. They were glad to make the sale.

Leona, just home from school

By this time I was about twelve years old and at the end of the school day when I came home, I would have a snack and then I went to work in the brewery. I had to hand pump the liquid from three barrels into the steel pressure tank. The pump was very large for me to handle. The corn or barley mash was run into the sewer as waste but on occasions, small portions of it we fed to the hogs. After my pumping job was done, we would do the farm chores, like milking, feeding the pigs and chickens etc.. We would then have supper.

After supper, Dad would go out to the workshop and get the stove going really good so the pressure in the tank would get up to a high temperature. He stayed near the stove so he could feed the fire. I was on the other side of the pressure tank where there was a gauge that I had to watch and when the gauge showed the correct temperature I let Dad know. The system for letting him know that the temperature was up to what it should be was for me to plug in an electric iron. Since the electric system we had was not very strong, whenever anything was plugged in, it would immediately make the lights burn dimmer. Anyone who remembers the early days of electricity knows what I am referring to. When homes first had electricity, whenever some appliance kicked in, the lights would flicker or burn just a little dimmer. I would plug in and then unplug the iron and he would know from the lights flickering that the temperature was right. Right next to the pressure tank was the livestock tank that held the cold water. There was a valve on the pressure tank and attached to the valve was a coil. The coil ran around and around in the tank. The valve on the pressure tank would be opened and vapor would flow through the coil. As the vapor flowed through the coil in the cold water it cooled and condensed back into liquid. The condensed liquid then passed through a spout at the end of the coil. It came out of the spout in a small steady stream. At this point I had to run it into jugs. This then was one hundred percent alcohol. The alcohol was tested at this time with an instrument that looked like a thermometer but it tested for the alcohol content. It had to be a hundred proof.

There was another way that moonshiners would test for the purity of the alcohol. They would take a tiny amount of the freshly brewed alcohol and put it in a saucer. They would then light a match and hold it over the saucer. The vapors from the moonshine in the saucer would burn with a blue flame and when it was all burned if there wasn't water left in the bottom of the saucer they knew they had a pure batch.

I helped with watching the temperature of the pressure tank, checking the proof and filling the jugs until 9:00 p.m. then my Mother came down and relieved me. My parents had fixed a spot for me to sleep there in the brewery until they went back up to the house much later. I would lie on some of the stacked sugar sacks while they continued to work. Sometimes my "bed" would be very high off the floor, other times it was quite low depending on how much sugar had been used and if there had been a recent delivery of sugar. If I had homework, I would do it then. About midnight they would finish and Dad would fill some of the charcoal barrels to set aside to start to age. When the liquor had aged the right length of time it would have a good taste. At that time the barrels were ready to be buried in the holes along the fence lines.

After Dad had set up the barrels for aging, it would finally be time to go up to the house. Dad would close up the trap door and we would head up to the house. My Mother who was a great cook would make a light lunch for us and then it was off to bed. One of the really good lunches she would make consisted of cooked onions with a little salt and pepper and then cream poured over the top. What a tasty snack that was!

We usually brewed about one or two times a week. On the nights that we didn't brew, the mash had to be set up. That meant that whatever kind of grain Dad was going to use was put into the three barrels, then the cakes of yeast and the sugar were put in, and last enough water to fill the barrel. That then was left to ferment.

I got very tired of my "night job." Pumping out the mash once or twice a week, filling the jugs or barrels, and helping to bury them was hard work for a twelve year old girl. It was a long day for me too. We would get up in the morning, do chores, I would go to school, come home, do chores, have supper and then help in the brewery. Then about midnight, sometimes later, we would head up to the house, have lunch, go to bed and the next morning start again. But that's just the way it was with families at that time. No matter whether the family was involved with farming, raising livestock or whatever, everyone in the family was expected to help out. Everyone had their chores. In order to survive and get all the work done, all hands were needed. So it wasn't unusual that as the oldest child in the family I was expected to help with making the whiskey. The bootlegging was a big part of making the money to put food on our table during hard times.

Rainy nights were the best time to bury the barrels and jugs in the holes along the fence line. It wasn't pleasant to be out there in the rain but it was a good time because we could open the holes, remove the wooden lid, drop the barrel or jugs in, replace the lid and cover it over with ground, and there would be no evidence that the ground had been disturbed. Since we always used the horses and wagon the rain also covered the tracks. The holes were of varying sizes. Some were large enough to hold a twenty gallon barrel, while others would hold only one or two of the one gallon jugs.

An amusing sidelight is that some jugs were forgotten. They were buried and my Dad forgot to take them out. These were some that were not buried in the wooden boxes. They had just been buried in the ground. He had used a post hole auger to make a hole deep enough to stack two-one gallon jugs and then covered dirt over the top. Long after my Dad had quit making whiskey, he and five other family members were out pheasant hunting one day. All of a sudden my uncle August called to Dad, "Look what I found!" Dad knew immediately what it must be. There sticking out of the ground were the necks of some bottles. They had been buried there in the alfalfa field for a long time and the dirt had eroded away. So instead of pheasants the men had hunted up some very well aged jugs of whiskey. They proceeded to enjoy the liquid refreshment and the pheasants in the fields got to live another day.

The agents had some idea that moonshiners were hiding whiskey in the ground. They carried long rods with them when they came to search. They would stick the long rods into the ground along fence lines and various other places. However, they never happened to find where any of our whiskey was hidden along the fence lines.

There was a day, during the whiskey making time that my Dad came into the house for dinner. He was very upset. He said, "We are really in big trouble!" He had just been down at the creek where the sewer emptied the mash into the water. The water in the creek was quite low and the sewer pipe was easily visible. There were a great number of very fat carp (fish) there. They were fighting like mad to get to the drain. They thought the mash was excellent fish food. They were also acting pretty tipsy. That many fat fish swimming around right by the drain would have been a dead give away to the Federal Agents if they would have happened to come along that day. They had been feeding there for some time before my Dad discovered the situation. He knew something would have to be done to remedy it. The first thing we did was to start catching a bunch of them. We caught plenty for several meals. But what to do with all the rest swimming around there?

Luck was with us though. Before we could do anything else we had a very heavy rain storm. There was so much rain that the creek went way out of its banks. As a result of the heavy rain the water around the drain was very deep and the sewer pipe was not exposed so you couldn't see the fish feeding anymore and that took care of that problem.

Sometimes during the day Dad would be working down in the brewing area of the barn. Mom and I had to be the look-outs for any cars coming into our yard. If anyone was coming in the driveway, my Mom would plug in and unplug the electric iron in the house two times. That, of course, would dim the lights or make the lights flicker over in the barn. Dad would know that someone was arriving in the yard. He would quickly close things up and go upstairs to the workshop area. It would appear that he was working on motors or blacksmithing.

One day my Father came home from town and said he had an order for a twenty gallon barrel of whiskey for a man from Sioux City. It was a stranger. My Dad had told the stranger that he would have to pay in cash. The deal was made for the following night. When the night came, my Dad got the horses and wagon ready. He said, "Leona, let's get it done."

We went out and dug up one of the barrels and loaded it in the wagon. We were working in the dark as we always did, so no one would see what we were doing. After it was loaded we drove about a half mile and all at once my Father said, "Whoa!" And we stopped. I said, "What is the matter?" Dad said, "You know I have this strange feeling. Let's unload the barrel here along the fence line in those long dry weeds and go home." I thought, "What a deal." We unloaded it and went home. We were home about an hour when the stranger arrived. The first thing Dad said to him was, "Do you have the cash?" The stranger handed Dad a bank draft from a Sioux City Bank. My Dad said, " I can't get you the stuff with that. It has to be cash." The stranger looked pretty upset and we thought he might put up a fight, but then he turned and left. The next morning Dad went to the bank in Parkston and asked the banker if that draft would have been good. The banker said "No, that bank recently closed." So thanks to Dad's "strange feeling" or premonition he avoided a loss.

12.
No More Brewing

Dad continued with his brewing for some time. Then he got in contact with a man and wife who were bootleggers from Sioux City, IA. He could buy liquor from them very reasonably and have it delivered to the farm. At this point Dad closed up his brewery and got rid of any evidence of his former whiskey making. He took the coil out of the water tank and buried it in the hillside. He started dealing with the people from Sioux City. They delivered pure alcohol and now Dad had a new project.

This one hundred percent pure alcohol came in one gallon cans. Dad took this alcohol and diluted it down with water. My Mother took white sugar and caramelized it until it was a nice shade of brown. The caramelized sugar was then added to each gallon that had been diluted. This resulted in a very good flavored whiskey. Dad created labels for his jugs and people really liked this whiskey and they would ask for it by label.

Here again, I had a part to play in getting this whiskey ready to sell. My job was to put the labels on each jug, an easier job than I had before.

One day my Dad had walked down the driveway to the mailbox to get the day's mail. The couple from Sioux City happened to arrive at the gate at the same time he did. Dad said they should drive on up to the house and he would be there shortly. Of course, they insisted that Dad jump in their little coupe and ride up with them. Dad looked at the little car and at the husband's very large wife and wondered to himself, how can we all fit? But since they were insisting that he ride with them, he suggested that the lady get out, let him get in and she could then sit on his lap. That's what was done. Dad said she was so heavy that even though she was on his lap, she was still sitting on the cushion. When they reached the house, she didn't get out of the car immediately. The three of them sat and talked for awhile in the car. When she finally did get up and get out of the car, Dad said he didn't know if his legs would support him because they had gone to sleep with all that weight on them. It took awhile before he could stand up. We laughed about that for a long time after.

13. The Big Disaster

Some time after Dad had quit brewing his own whiskey and had buried the coil and cleaned up all the equipment the big disaster struck. The Federal Agents appeared again. They first went to Dad's brother, August's, farm and searched there and then left. August had a feeling that they were heading to our farm so he telephoned to warn us.

We had plenty of time to clear up everything and cover our tracks before they drove into the yard. As they started searching, they told Dad, "we know where you are brewing the alcohol but we don't know how to get down there." They were referring to the area under the barn where we were no longer making any whiskey. They continued to search for the entrance for a long time with no luck. They could not find anything.

Then they cornered me and tried to get me to tell where it was or if we had any whiskey. But I wouldn't talk. I had been well coached for a long time about never telling anything that we were doing. Even now, I remember how frightened I was.

They finally gave up with me but then they talked to Dad again. "We know there is a secret entrance here someplace and if you don't talk and we can't locate it, we have the authority to blow up the building" So Dad opened up and showed them the trap door and they went down. Dad didn't think there was any evidence down there anymore.

Everything had been cleaned up and was no longer being used. The coil had been taken out a long time ago and buried in the hillside, but of course, he didn't tell them that. They did find one thing; somehow, accidentally one gallon of whiskey had been left down there. Finding that gallon of whiskey, gave them the right to demolish everything down there so there would be no chance of it ever being used again as a brewery.

They smashed all the fifty gallon barrels that had been used for mash but that were now all cleaned up. They broke all the five, ten and fifteen gallon crocks along with the stock tank. Everything down there was in pieces, completely destroyed.

When they got to the upright hundred gallon steel tank Dad begged them not to demolish it. He planned to move that out and use it as a storage tank for gasoline. Surprisingly, they did not destroy it.

While they were busy breaking everything else down there, the noise of all the breakage was deafening. At this time Ewald, the hired man, who knew nothing about the whiskey operation, came home from the field with the horses. It was always my job to help him with the horses when he came back from the field. The horses had to be watered and then taken into a barn. When Ewald heard all the smashing and crashing sounds, he couldn't imagine what was going on. I told him, "They finally found the place." But Ewald didn't understand what I was talking about. When we finished taking care of the horses, he walked over to where all the noise was coming from. He couldn't believe his eyes. He couldn't believe that this operation had been going on all the time and he didn't know anything about it. He had never been told about it so that he could never be put on the spot or accused of having anything to do with it. He commented that he was usually dead tired by the time he came in from the field. Eating and then getting to bed were his main thoughts.

Dad was arrested for the gallon of whiskey that had been found and his punishment was a fine and thirty days in the Hutchinson County jail.

The Federal Agents had also found a small amount of whiskey at Uncle August's farm so he was arrested and went to jail as well.

I remember Ewald taking Mom and me to the county jail at Olivet on Sunday afternoons to visit Dad and August. Ewald would also discuss with Dad how the farming operation should proceed and what he should do each week.

There was one other person in jail. Some days the jailer would take the three inmates down to the James River to fish.

14. Return from Jail

After Dad was released from jail, he did remove the large steel tank from the basement of the barn and used it for gasoline for many years.

In later years, a fire destroyed the barn., so Dad put a roof over the basement and continued to use it but not for moonshine anymore.

The farm, the low building near the big horse barn is the building that had burned and Dad put a roof over the basement. The basement where the third brewery had been

My dad had quit the moonshine business, but that didn't mean that his name wasn't used by other people who were selling moonshine. He had a reputation for making excellent whiskey and so some people would sell their moonshine saying, "This is some of Adolph Schelske's moonshine." Though it wasn't true it did help their sales. Unfortunately some of the whiskey falsely advertised and sold as being made by him, was really rotten stuff. But there wasn't anything he could do about it. After about two years it finally stopped.

Though alcohol was always readily available around our home none of our family ever developed a problem with over indulgence. The federal revenue agents were still around but they had their eye on others now.

15. Home Searches

During the prohibition era the Federal Revenue Agents searched many homes. They took their job seriously and patrolled heavily. They would frequently make surprise visits to people's homes and many families were not brewing liquor to sell, they were making only enough for their own families. People didn't want to get caught with any liquor during any of the searches so they became very creative in hiding their "home brew."

Revenue Agents arrived at the farm home of one family that we knew that kept only a little liquor in the house for their own consumption. The day the Federal Agents appeared at their farm, there was no time to hide anything. They had one gallon of whiskey in the pantry. They also had a small baby in a cradle in the kitchen. In those days the women wore long dresses and aprons and with quick thinking the mother took the baby in her arms, grabbed the jug of whiskey and sat down in a chair. She placed the jug on the floor by the chair and fanned her long skirt around and over it. She remained seated there, hiding the jug and holding the baby all the while the agents were searching; the gallon jug of moonshine was never found thanks to her cool head and quick thinking.

In some homes the hiding place was in the center pedestal of the big wooden kitchen table. The center pedestal would be hollowed out enough so that a quart jar would fit in it. The table top covered the hollowed out area so it served quite well as a hiding place. To retrieve the jar, you would pull the table apart as though you were putting in one of the table leaves.

Another gentleman hid his liquor in the stairway. One step was fixed so that he could hide a jar or jug in it.

By 1933, it had become very evident that prohibition was not working and wasn't solving any of the problems they had hoped it would. The government finally accepted the fact that prohibition was a failure and it was repealed. People didn't have to go through all this secretiveness and hiding anymore if they wanted to enjoy a glass of spirits.

Epilogue

After his thirty day jail term, my dad gave up all moonshine activities. He continued farming and I became his right-hand assistant with that.

He also did overhaul and repair of stationary engines for neighboring farmers in that same barn where the basement had housed the still. Along with the engine repair, he sharpened sickles for grass mowers for other farmers. That was a sideline business that he did in his spare time. He had plenty of customers because he was fair and lenient with his charges for the work. If the customer did not have the money to pay when the job was completed Dad would say, "Just pay me when you can or when you sell some of your crops." His sideline business was good for him and good for the neighbors. It was something he could do in his spare time and it brought in some extra money. For the neighbors it was good because they didn't have to pay immediately if they were short on cash and they were always very grateful.

Leona as a young lady, sitting on a cistern. In the background is the sod house, which in later years had siding put on.

ADOLPH SCHELSKE, PRESIDENT
THEODORE PIETZ, VICE PRESIDENT
EDWARD BADER, SECRETARY

LEO WINTER, TREASURER
HERBERT BARTEL, CLERK
WM. FIEDLER, ENGINEER

NU-ANGLE

NU-ANGLE JACK COMPANY

PARKSTON, SOUTH DAKOTA

Top of the stationary for Nu-Angle Jack Company.

In addition to his farming, and his custom repair work, he found some time to invent a new kind of car jack for use in changing tires. He and a partner worked for some time developing a hydraulic jack. They did a great deal of experimenting with different designs and models. After much hard work and the expenditure of several thousand dollars they felt they had a good workable jack.

They then proceeded to get a patent on their design. The jack was called "Nu-Angle Lifting Jack." and their business was named "Nu-Angle Jack Company" address: Parkston, SD. Their stationery listed the following names and positions: Adolph Schelske, President; Theodore Pietz, Vice President; Edward Bader, Secretary; Leo Winter, Treasurer; Herbert Bartel, Clerk; and William Fiedler, engineer.

They set about having the jack manufactured in Minneapolis, MN. The year was 1935 and there was a need for this type of jack for changing the frequent flat tires and blow outs that occurred with the early-day autos.

Although it was an excellent jack, cash flow problems developed. Even with the financial help of shareholders they were not able to continue with the manufacturing.

After all the hard work of developing, experimenting, getting the patent, finding a manufacturer, and marketing they were forced to

This jack may be placed under either the front or rear wheel from either side of the wheel, that is, it may be used either right or left hand. And a further advantage may be had when you encounter a flat or blow-out either on an up-hill or down-grade, because blow-outs don't ask the motorist when he wants them to show up—they just happen and there you are. In such an event you simply leave your car in low or reverse gear to hold it from rolling away. You do not need to lock the brakes because it may interfere with removing the wheel in most cases, so you just leave your car in gear. Place your Nu-Angle jack under the respective axle from the down-hill side, that is, you shove the jack up-hill under the car. You can do this with a Nu-Angle, because it can be used either right hand or left hand. Then you proceed to raise your car as already described elsewhere in this pamphlet. The base or bottom member of the jack will hold the down-hill pressure of the car even if you raise up a rear wheel without any brakes set. The jack will hold the car from rolling away under the most severe circumstances. It has been done many times, and can be done again by anyone. "Whatever man has done men can do."

Experience has shown us that ordinary lifting jacks and the new, underslung, low streamlined cars leave the motorist in a rather difficult situation when it comes to changing a flat tire to a good spare, and that when many miles away from the good Samaritan service man of the large city. Then is the time that every motorist wishes he had a reliable and efficient lifting jack, one that he could depend upon and that he could do the job himself instead of possibly sending a message many miles for a service man to come out and change his tire. Well, you may say you would drive a flat to the next service station. Very well, but even if you did sacrifice a good tire and possibly a wheel you may not be able to do it at that. There are more than one reason why you cannot drive a flat tire a great distance.

The automobile industry has made wonderful strides in the last few years in improving the speed of our cars; also the safety factor has received considerable attention. One of our new, modern cars may be rolled over several times without injuring anyone, though I suggest no one but an experienced proving

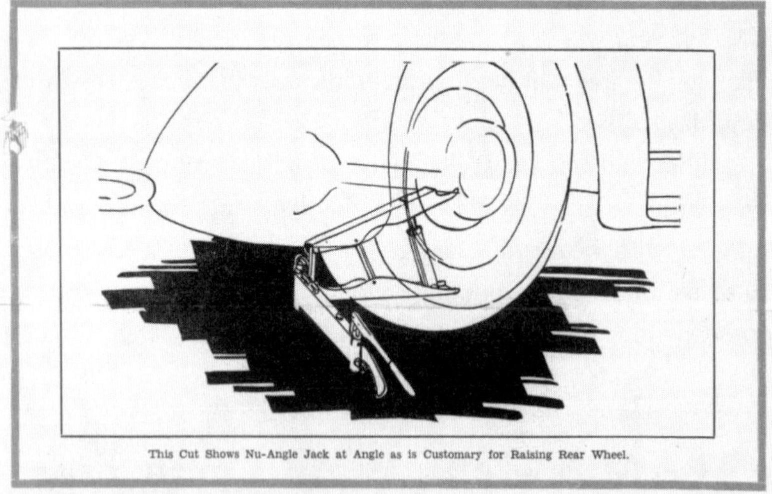

This Cut Shows Nu-Angle Jack at Angle as is Customary for Raising Rear Wheel.

ground man should try it. But we have not heard of a car yet that had absolutely blow-out proof and flat proof tires. We still have blow-outs and flats once in a while. And as far as we know, we will continue to have flats, more or less. Therefore, we should be prepared at all times to meet the issue.

In spite of all the wonderful improvements the auto industry has made, little attention has been given the problem of changing wheels or tires and to equip our modern cars with the best, most reliable and fool proof means of raising a wheel for such a change.

This problem has been left entirely to accessory and lifting jack manufacturers, and we admit that they have done all they could, but yet, that didn't get us very far. We have found that something better, more efficient, more secure was needed, and now we have the answer.

Sample brochure from Nu-Angle Jack Company

THE NU-ANGLE LIFTING JACK

The Nu-Angle Jack Company is proud at this time to announce to the auto-minded public that this most UNDESIRABLE task of raising up a car to make a change of a wheel or tire is now fully solved.

To place and locate a Nu-Angle lifting jack under your car you do not have to soil you good clothes, get your hands and face scratched, and in some cases even religion has to suffer a little, especially if it be on a Sunday morning on your way to church. Yes, blow-outs and flat tires have no respect for church or religion. They are always present.

The accompanying cuts show two different ways or positions in which this new lifting jack may be used or applied, but the different applications and uses are so many-fold that it would require a great number of cuts if we were going to try to picture them all.

The Nu-Angle Lifting Jack meets a long felt want. It serves the small garages very well. It is the ideal thing for the service station and the tire shop. It is indispensible to the motorist who ventures out onto our highways and by-ways where he is far removed from his faithful service man or trouble shooter.

Tourists cannot aford to ignore this new and unique lifting jack on their long journeys through the Bad Lands and places unknown to them, but where they may want to go out of curiosity where the motorists' nightmare, the blow-out and flat tire, will follow them and is always, so to speak, riding the rear bumper wherever they go.

The Nu-Angle Lifting Jack retails to anyone for the small sum of $11.95, and South Dakota 3% sales tax, plus a small transportation charge from Parkston, South Dakota.

HISTORY OF NU-ANGLE JACK

The Nu-Angle Jack was not discovered by mere accident or luck, but much rather is the fruit of several years of hard labor in experimenting with different designs and models to bring it to its present state of perfection. Besides much experimenting and hard work, several thousand dollars in solid, hard cash were spent to produce this product but already we feel well repaid for our time, effort and money in the result of this new, unique, and perfect model.

"Necessity is the mother of inventions" is rather an old saying, but it surely packs a whole lot of truth.

So, likewise, is the Nu-Angle Jack the result of necessity.

In the year 1935, the inventor of the Nu-Angle Jack, just a common poor man who at that time owned an Essex Coach of the Underslung type, poor tires with plenty of flats and blow outs made frequent changes a regular routine, and that with a common lifting jack. So he had to go through all the unpleasant tasks of crawling under muddy bumpers and fenders to set a lifting jack. This ruined clothes, soiled shirt sleeves, scratched hands, and even the face did suffer scratches that led to the designing of a lifting jack that could be placed under a car successfully without all the unpleasant details above mentioned. That was the beginning of the history of the Nu-Angle Lifting Jack.

For your convenience we have attached an order blank to this circular. Just tear off along the dotted line, fill in your name and address and enclose money order or bank draft. Do not send personal checks or cash in your letter.

You may if you wish, send just $2.00 with your order and pay the balance to your postmaster upon receipt of your Nu-Angle Lifting Jack. But by remitting the full amount with your order you save the C. O. D. charges.

If you want to be so kind, after reading this circular, you may hand it to a neighbor or friend.

Very respectfully,
THE NU-ANGLE JACK COMPANY
Parkston, South Dakota.

The enclosed cuts in this pamphlet are intended to give you a fair idea what the Nu-Angle Jack looks like, since you have not had the privilege of seeing an actual working model, thought it is rather a hard problem to do justice in describing it. This jack is built along smooth, streamlined lines and is a beauty of mechanical art for the eye to behold, and it is every bit as efficient, and more so than it looks.

The Nu-Angle Jack is of the hydraulic, or liquid force action, type. This is the most powerful means of expansion known to mechanical science.

The Nu-Angle lifting jack is manufactured under Patent No. 2,031,700. Patented Feb. 25, 1936. This patent is now soley owned and controlled by the Nu-Angle Jack Co.

TEAR OFF ON DOTTED LINE

ORDER BLANK

NU-ANGLE JACK COMPANY, Parkston, S. D.

Ship by.................................this order for.................................

Nu-Angle Jacks, Amount $.................................Cash enclosed, $.................................

Ship C. O. D. Balance of $.................................

Name ....Address ....

Sample brochure from Nu-Angle Jack Company

give up the dream. That was a heart breaker for everyone involved.

Even more disheartening was the fact that after the patent expired, their design of the jack was picked up by another company. With a minimum of changes, that company successfully produced the jack and it is still in existence. If only the "Nu-Angle Jack" company could have raised the additional money when cash flow problems developed, it would

Leona demonstrating the use of the jack while changing a tire

In the foreground is the hydraulic jack that Adolph and a partner invented and then patented in 1936, in the background is the two-story house we lived in and to the left is the sod house where Grandpa and Grandma lived

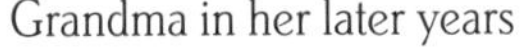

Grandma in her later years

Adolph and Emelia in later years standing by their car in front of their house

have been produced under their name and they would have reaped the profits from it.

Dad then devoted himself to the farming, custom repair work, and custom trucking of livestock to the Sioux Falls, SD, and Sioux City, IA, livestock markets.

And my three brothers provided a sideline interest for him when they formed their band, "Little Elmer's Accordion Band." Dad had always loved music so he really enjoyed going to the dances they played for. I'm sure it brought back memories for him of when he was a young man and he had played his fiddle for dances.

According to information on the website of the South Dakota Fraternal Order of Police the revenue agent I referred to as Mr. X., who often searched our farm, was killed in 1927 by a moonshiner in the northern part of South Dakota.

Mr. X. had gone with several other agents to investigate reports that a man near Redfield, SD, was a bootlegger. One of the officers tried to arrest the alleged bootlegger on a prohibition charge, but the suspect shot and wounded the officer.

The suspect then fled and was found hiding in a barn. Mr. X. and another federal agent went into the barn where the suspect shot and killed both agents. The suspect then fled again and went to a straw stack where he fatally shot himself.

As for Ewald, the hired hand who had helped with the farming during the moonshine days, he continued to work for dad for a few more years. During those years he married and some time after that he got his own farm. He and his bride had a family and remained close friends of our family.

Ed, who had been Dad's assistant with the moonshine operation, graduated from high school with a great reputation for his athletic talents. He and his basketball teammates won the 1925 state tournament for Parkston. He did go on to college using the money he had earned on the farm and later married and had a family.

My Mom was kept busy with the family. By this time there were four children which included a set of twins.

As for me, being the oldest in the family, it fell to me to become Dad's hired hand on the farm, especially after Ewald acquired his own farm. Shocking grain, pitching bundles, hauling hay, feeding the livestock, milking cows was all in a day's work. This continued until I married and moved away to start my own family.

It's a story that needed to be told
So that in our memories
we might hold
Those people and times
that came before
And so that history
might live forever more.

By Sharon Schnabel